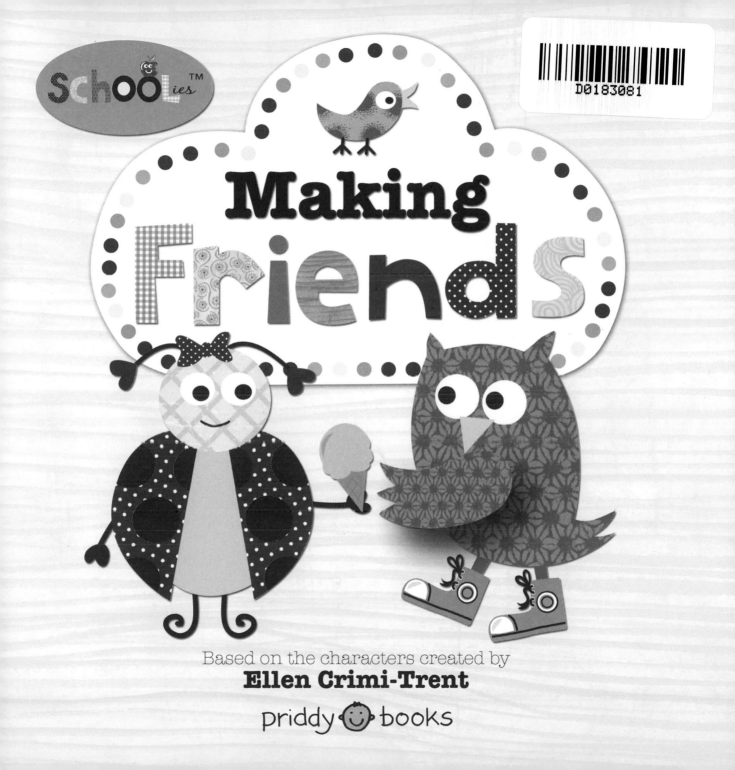

Making Friends

Based on the characters created by
Ellen Crimi-Trent

priddy books

Leeza was a very loud Schoolie.
Her twin sister Lydia, was a shy Schoolie.

At school, when Leeza sat with her friends,
Lydia felt too shy to join them.

One day, Mrs Meow told the Schoolies that it was Friendship Week. This was a special week all about friendship.

Lydia drooped.
She felt too shy to be friendly.

Mrs Meow set a jar on her desk.
She called it the Friendship Jar.

Lydia drooped a bit more.
She didn't think that she would get
any notes in the Friendship Jar.

At lunch, Lydia took an empty
seat beside Spencer.

Lydia noticed Spencer wasn't eating.
She straightened up and spoke,
but no louder than a whisper.

Lydia opened her lunch box,
and offered to share.

After eating lunch, they decided they would sit together again.

At play time, Lydia sat alone, beneath her
favourite tree, to read her favourite book.

BAM! The tree shook,
and leaves fell.

Poor Zippy, the fastest Schoolie at Angler Primary, had crashed into Lydia's tree!

Lydia took Zippy to see Mrs Fox,
the school nurse.

Then it was time for music class.
Mrs Hedge played piano while the Schoolies
played musical instruments or sang.

Hayden couldn't follow the beat on his drum.

Lydia clapped in time to the beat of the music so Hayden could follow along.

Soon Hayden was tapping his drum in time to the music.

Lydia's happy heart seemed to
beat in time to the music.
She began to sing.

Everyone heard a wonderful voice.

At the end of the day, Mrs Meow was surprised to see so many notes in the Friendship Jar.

Mrs Meow read the notes out loud.
They were all for Lydia!

Lydia blushed. She smiled, and in a quiet, but very clear voice, she spoke.